Last of the Tsars

D1343227

PANORAMA OF HISTORY SERIES

This series has been created to provide a vivid portrayal of major events
in world history. Each text is concise but authoritative, giving essential
facts combined with an insight into the character of the period and
people involved. Every book includes a large number of full-colour
illustrations and many more in black and white, all researched from
contemporary sources; these paintings, prints, maps and photographs all
carry informative captions and are carefully integrated with the text.
Published simultaneously with this volume is THE BATTLE OF
TRAFALGAR, and two more titles — THE SPANISH ARMADA and
THE INDUSTRIAL REVOLUTION — will be published in April, 1972.
Further 'Panoramas' will be added to the series at regular intervals.

Last of the Tsars

The Life and Death of Nicholas and Alexandra
Richard Tames

Pan Books

Panorama of History Series

First published 1972 by Pan Books Ltd, 33 Tothill Street, London, SW1.

ISBN 0 330 02902 9

PICTURE CREDITS
BPC LIBRARY 14/15
CAMERA PRESS LIMITED 7
CIVICHE RACCOLTE D'ARTE APPLICATA ED INCISIONI, MILAN 39
CONTEMPORARY FILMS LIMITED 62
MR HANS TASIEMKA 31,37
THE IMPERIAL WAR MUSEUM 44, 52, 63
THE MANSELL COLLECTION 9, 12, 19, 21, 21, 24, 32, 35, 40, 43,
    56, 57
NOVOSTI PRESS AGENCY Front Cover, 25, 27, 28/29, 44, 53, 55,
    58/59
PAN BOOKS LIMITED 3, 8
POPPERFOTO Inside Front Cover, 41, 46, 56
RADIO TIMES HULTON PICTURE LIBRARY 10, 13, 18, 20, 23, 32,
    33, 34, 36, 38, 42, 45, 46, 49, 50, 54, 55, 56, 60
SOCIETY FOR CULTURAL RELATIONS WITH THE USSR 11, 61, 64
THE WALTERS ART GALLERY, BALTIMORE 17

Printed in Great Britain by
Cox & Wyman Ltd, London, Fakenham and Reading

Contents

Note

The titles *Emperor* and *Tsar* are both correct and are used inter-changeably in this book. *Emperor* was a higher rank, first taken by Peter the Great, but Nicholas II, a Slavophile, preferred the older, more Russian title. *Tsar*.

Every Russian has three names: his first or Christian name; the name of his father with *vich* added (meaning son of); and his family name. Thus, Nicholas was Nicholas Alexandrovich Romanov. For women, the second name is their father's with *evna* or *ovna* (daughter of) added. The Tsar's youngest daughter was Anastasia Nicolaevna.

As the Imperial Eagle was symbolic of the autocratic power of the Tsars, so the Ikon was the symbol of the Orthodox Church's spiritual authority over the Russian Empire.

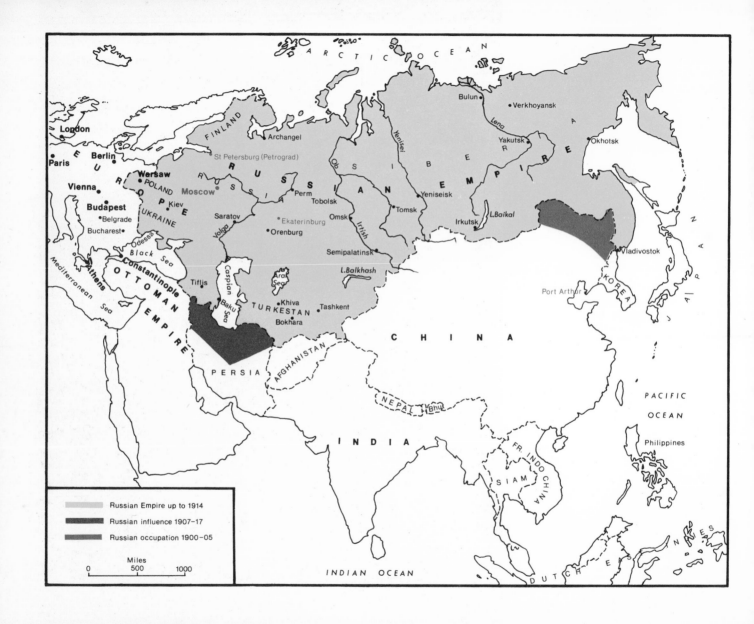

ARCTIC OCEAN

FINLAND

London
Paris
Berlin
Vienna
Budapest
Belgrade
Bucharest
Athens

Archangel
St Petersburg (Petrograd)
POLAND
Wersaw
Moscow
Kiev
UKRAINE
Odessa
Black Sea
Constantinople
Tiflis

RUSSIA
Perm
Saratov
Volga
Ekaterinburg
Orenburg
Caspian Sea
Baku
Aral Sea

Tobolsk
Omsk
Semipalatinsk
Irtish
L.Balkhash

Ob

Yenisei

RUSSIAN

Tomsk
Yeniseisk
Irkutsk
L.Baikal

SIBERIA

EMPIRE

Bulun
Verkhoyansk
Yakutsk
Lena
R

Okhotsk

Vladivostok

Mediterronean Sea

OTTOMAN EMPIRE

TURKESTAN
Khiva
Bokhara
Tashkent

PERSIA
AFGHANISTAN

CHINA

KOREA

Port Arthur

J
A
P
A
N

PACIFIC
OCEAN

Philippines

NEPAL
Bhu

INDIA

FR. INDO CHINA
SIAM

INDIAN OCEAN

DUTCH
E
S
N
D
I
E
S

Russian Empire up to 1914
Russian influence 1907–17
Russian occupation 1900–05

Miles
0   500   1000

1 The Empire of the Tsars

Stretching from the Baltic to the Pacific, from the Arctic to the borders of India, Persia and China, the Tsar's dominions were so vast that, as night began to fall along their western frontiers, dawn was already breaking on their Pacific coast. The Empire was less a country than a continent and its population was as varied as its scenery — not only Russians, Afghans, Uzbeks and Tartars but also Ukrainians, Poles, Finns, Balts, Jews, Lapps, Germans, Georgians and Armenians, making in all about 130,000,000 souls.

Four out of five of the Tsar's subjects were peasants, country dwellers freed from serfdom in 1861 by the Tsar-Liberator Alexander II, but still wretchedly poor and condemned by their rapidly rising numbers to even greater poverty. Their enemies were the landowners, the local officials and the Cossacks who collected the taxes and rents, but not the *Batiushka-Tsar,* the

Famine in Russia in the 1890s. Peasants take thatch from the roof of a hut to feed their livestock. The agricultural policy of the government was one of 'Export *and* die . . .'

Little Father, whose portrait was venerated like a Holy Ikon, God's representative on earth with the power of life and death.

Railways were gradually breaking down rural isolation, bringing new goods, new fasions, new ideas, opening up the eastern frontier to conquest and settlement, just as the Transcontinental Railroad had opened up the West in America. Russia's lifeline, the Trans-Siberian Railway, came thirty years after America's, but when completed it was even longer, stretching more than 4,000 miles from Moscow to Vladivostock. By the 1890s Russian society was beginning to feel the impact of the revolutions in transport and industry which had already transformed Western Europe.

Moscow before the Revolution, a view of the Kremlin from University Bridge. A French visitor described this 16th-century citadel as a living symbol of the Tsarist regime: 'This curious jumble of palaces, towers, churches, monasteries, chapels, barracks, arsenals and bastions; this incoherent mass of sacred and secular buildings; this mixture of functions as fortress, sanctuary, seraglio, harem, necropolis and orison; this blend of advanced civilization and archaic barbarism; this violent conflict of crudest materialism and most lofty spirituality; are they not the whole history of Russia, the whole epic of the Russian nation?'

St Petersburg

Moscow was the Empire's most important city, but not its capital. It was the hub from which the railways and waterways radiated as arteries of trade and commerce. It was 'The City of Forty Times Forty Churches', the Holy City, successor to Byzantium and Rome, the centre of the Orthodox faith and the seat of its greatest shrines. Two hundred miles to the north lay the capital, St Petersburg, the creation of Tsar Peter the Great (1681–1725), built on nineteen islands at the cost of 200,000 lives. Catherine the Great adorned it with palaces and public buildings in the Italian style to make it the 'Venice of the North'. It was the centre of the cultural and social life of the nobility, the home of the ballet and opera, the setting for duels and love affairs, balls and receptions. Here French, not Russian, was the language of society, and here, in the least Russian of all Russia's cities, the Tsar of all the Russias kept his court.

St Petersburg, Italianate capital of the Russian Empire, an island of European culture in a continent of Asiatic superstition.

2 The reign of Alexander III (1881-94)

Queen Victoria (in her curious use of the third person) once remarked that Alexander III was 'a sovereign who she does not look upon as a gentleman'. To his contemporaries he seemed to resemble a great Russian bear — powerful, gruff, narrow and suspicious. He was 6 foot 4 inches tall and immensely strong, capable of straightening horse-shoes and bending forks into knots. He had a passion for hunting and everything Russian — food, music, clothes, manners — and a dislike for pageantry, Englishmen and Germans. He towered over his Empire and his family alike. His sons enjoyed little independence and his ministers and officials went timidly about their business, because, as one said, when he spoke he 'gave the impression of being on the point of striking you'.

Alexander was the Autocrat of Russia and he ruled autocratically. There was no parliament to restrain him or question his actions and he sincerely believed that he was answerable only to God for his

Alexander III, Tsar of Russia — a rather idealized portrait in the year before his death.

policies. Ministers were appointed and dismissed by him alone; according to his will they could be sent into exile or pardoned for the gravest misdemeanours. A despot by temperament, Alexander was also a tyrant by conviction. His father, the Tsar-Liberator Alexander II, had been assassinated by revolutionary terrorists. The son determined to brook no opposition — hundreds of political suspects, liberals as much as radicals, were isolated in Siberia; heavy censorship muffled the Press; spies and secret police kept close watch on students and intellectuals.

A reactionary in politics, Alexander was progressive in many other ways. He made a military alliance with friendless France and thus was able to borrow heavily on the Paris Bourse to finance his massive programme of railway construction. He re-equipped the Army, but resisted all temptations to drag Russia into war. He encouraged foreign capitalists to develop Russia's coal and iron deposits and he put the national finances on a sound footing. In 1894, the year of his death, he was forty-nine, and apparently at the height of his powers. The Empire was safe, the dynasty secure, great things were expected of the next decade. Already there were those who believed this vigorous ruler might one day stand beside Peter the Great or Ivan the Terrible. His heir, the Tsarevich Nicholas, was, if not neglected, at least largely forgotten.

The Tsarevich

Nicholas, for his part, was happy to remain in the background. He stood in awe of his father and was all too conscious of his own abilities, or rather the lack of them. He was gentle, shy, good-natured and heir to the Imperial throne by default. Of Alexander's four sons, one (also named Alexander) died in infancy, while the second, George, was a

The playboy prince — Tsarevich Nicholas II in the uniform of a cavalry officer. Notice the eagle-crested helmet in his right hand.

tubercular semi-invalid living in seclusion in the Caucasus. Nicholas accordingly became Tsarevich, heir to the throne, and was brought up in spartan simplicity in the 900-room palace at Gatchina. As a child he slept on an Army cot, took a cold bath each morning and ate the peasant diet of his father. His education was largely in the hands of one man — Constantine Petrovich Pobedonostsev. This aged professor of law from Moscow University was a staunch defender of reactionary politics. He taught Nicholas that the Slavs were an idle, stupid people who needed strong leadership, that only autocracy and the Orthodox religion could give unity and strength to the Tsar's sprawling Empire, and that constitutions and parliaments were evil and corrupt. As a child, Nicholas had been brought to the bedside of the mangled, dying Alexander II, the liberal reformer who fell victim to the seventh attempt on his life. Nicholas received from his tutors the precepts of reaction, from his father the practice. Obedient and willing he determined to follow where they led.

By the age of twenty-one Nicholas was a slim youth of five foot seven inches. He was charming and friendly in a quiet way. His education was excellent; he had an unusually good memory, spoke French and German with ease and his English was so faultless he might have been taken for an Englishman. He rode well, danced gracefully and was a first class shot. In May 1890, a few days before his twenty-second birthday he wrote in his diary, 'today I finished definitely and for ever my educa-

tion' and henceforth he directed his energies to becoming a playboy prince. He rose late, usually with a hangover, attended dreary official meetings for form's sake, then escaped to hunting, ice-skating or a military review. The evenings were filled with dinners, balls, plays, opera — and the ballet, where he met Mathilde Kschessinska, a vivacious and brilliant seventeen-year-old ballerina who responded eagerly to the attentions of the Tsarevich, knowing well that an 'arrangement' rather than marriage was all she could ever hope for.

Partly to end this liaison, partly to complete his education, Nicholas was bundled off on a world tour in October 1890 with his brother George and their cousin Prince George of Greece. By the time they reached the Nile the battleship *Pamiat Azova* had become a travelling house party and the three princes began to enjoy themselves thoroughly — climbing the pyramids, riding camels and watching naked belly dancers. India was disappointing by comparison — tedious formalities and the 'stifling' English. Thereafter they continued eastwards but the tour halted abruptly in Japan when an assassin swung at Nicholas with a samurai sword and

The governor of Kursk in processsion 1883 — a painting by the Russian artist Repin. Notice the holy ark, banners, priests, police and cripples. The mixture of military uniforms, European dress, clerical vestments and native costume shows the strange compound of influences which made up the Russian way of life.

gashed open his forehead. Prince George of Greece parried a second blow but Nicholas was scarred for life and with the scar carried an enduring dislike of the Japanese, whom he referred to as 'monkeys'. The attempted assassination has never been explained.

Returning to St Petersburg Nicholas resumed his affair with Mathilde Kschessinska. He sent her flowers, met her in secret; and he gave her a gold bracelet studded with diamonds. He began to visit her dressing-room at the opera house. When she rented a house from the composer Rimsky-Korsakov, Nicholas became a regular visitor. He still performed numerous official functions — presiding energetically over a famine relief committee, attending the meetings of the Finance Committee and acting as president of the Trans-Siberian Railway. Mathilde, by now a protégée of the great Tchaikovsky, became increasingly a mere distraction. More and more Nicholas began to think of Alix.

Alix

Alix Victoria Helena Louise Beatrice, Princess of Hesse-Darmstadt was born on June 6th, 1872, in the medieval Rhineland city of Darmstadt. Named after her mother, Princess Alice of England, the third of Queen Victoria's nine children, she was 'a sweet, merry little person, always laughing and soon nicknamed Sunny'. As a member of the large international family dominated by 'Granny', Queen Victoria, Alix's upbringing was English. Mrs Orchard, her English governess, decreed fresh air, exercise, regular habits and rice puddings, and every year the family visited Queen Victoria at Balmoral, Osborne or Windsor. As she grew up Alix showed great talent for the piano and, for a woman, an unusual interest in politics.

Nicholas first saw her as a child of twelve at the wedding of her sister Ella to Grand Duke Serge. Five years later, in 1889, she visited Ella for six weeks and the Tsarevich, now twenty-one, became her constant companion.

'My dream is some day to marry Alix H. I have loved her a long while and still deeper and stronger since 1889', Nicholas confided to his diary in 1892, not daring to hope that his dream could come true. Alix had not made a good impression in Russia. To the sophisticated ladies of St Petersburg society she seemed a gawky, provincial adolescent — badly dressed, an awkward dancer and with an appalling French accent. It was safe to snipe at her because both Tsar Alexander and Empress Marie were strongly anti-German and planned to marry the Tsarevich not to the younger daughter of a petty princeling, but to Hélène, daughter of the Comte de Paris, Pretender to the throne of France. There was, moreover, the obstacle of religion. Alix was a fervent Protestant; a Russian Empress would have to become a member of the Orthodox Church. Only one person was adamant that all obstacles could be overcome and a marriage arranged —

Nicholas.

Alexander ignored Nicholas' whims, hoping the boy would lose interest amid the distractions of society and the demands of court life. Then, in 1894, the Tsar was suddenly wracked with influenza and nephritis, a disease of the kidneys. His energy ebbed alarmingly. Concern for his future led to concern for his heir and his country. A marriage had to be arranged and Nicholas was given leave to propose to Alix at the forthcoming wedding of her older brother Ernest, now Grand Duke of Hesse-Darmstadt.

Engagement

At Coburg, where the royalty of Europe had gathered for the wedding, Nicholas pressed his suit with ardour but without success. 'We talked till twelve, but with no result; she still objects to changing her religion. Poor girl, she cried a lot.' Nicholas noted in his diary. Then 'Granny' came to his aid. Queen Victoria favoured a brilliant marriage for her favourite grand-daughter and, in a confidential talk, persuaded the reluctant Alix that Orthodoxy was not *so* different from Lutheranism. The next day Alix gave Nicholas her consent. It was, he wrote, 'A marvellous, unforgettable day . . . O God what a mountain has rolled from my shoulders . . . The whole day I have been walking in a dream without fully realizing what was happening to me . . . The whole family was simply enraptured . . . I cannot even believe that I

am engaged . . .'

A flood of congratulatory telegrams followed the announcement of the news. Empress Marie sent Alix an emerald bracelet and a gem-studded Easter egg. 'It seems that everybody in Russia has sent flowers to my fiancée,' Nicholas recorded ecstatically; and then proudly wrote to his mother that Alix had just written 'two sentences in Russian without error'.

In June Nicholas and Alix went to England. After three blissful days in a secluded country retreat, they joined 'Granny' at Windsor, where a gift from Tsar Alexander awaited Alix — a *sautoir* of pearls valued at 250,000 gold roubles, executed by Fabergé, the court jeweller. Granny, having played the part of matchmaker, 'even allowed us to go for drives without a chaperone'. Nicholas and Alix were chosen as godparents for a new-born prince 'a nice healthy child', who would one day become Edward VIII and later Duke of Windsor. The idyllic six weeks ended in July but Alix and Nicholas were soon reunited under very different circumstances.

An Easter egg by Fabergé the court jeweller. This gold and pearl masterpiece contains a model of the Gatchina Palace, where Nicholas was brought up.

'I am not prepared to be a Tsar'

In September the Tsar, having apparently recovered from his illness, suffered a sudden relapse and was rushed to the warmth of Livadia, the Imperial summer palace in the Crimea. Father John of Kronstadt, a miracle-worker, prayed at his bedside while a specialist from Vienna hovered around the still truculent patient. Alix rushed to be with Nicholas, and the dying Tsar insisted on meeting her in full-dress uniform and sealing in person their formal betrothal. It was his last act of state. Ten days later he died and Nicholas succeeded him.

To the grief of the bereaved the new Tsar added the anxiety of a young man faced with awesome responsibilities. To his brother-in-law Grand Duke Alexander he confessed, 'I am not prepared to be a Tsar. I never wanted to become one. I know nothing of the business of ruling. I have no idea of even how to talk to the ministers'. Alix had already become his chief source of strength. In his first Imperial Decree he proclaimed her new faith, title and name as 'the truly believing Grand Duchess Alexandra Fedorovna' and she stood beside him through the first week of mourning at Livadia, during the endless rail journey to St Petersburg, at the memorial services in Kharkov, Kursk, Orel and Tula and the ten litanies in the solemn procession through Moscow. The ceremonies reached their climax in St Petersburg where sixty-one royal personages gathered to witness the entombment of Tsar Alexander III in the Cathedral of the Fortress of Peter and Paul, the resting place of the Romanovs.

A week later Nicholas and Alexandra were married, on the birthday of Marie, now the Dowager Empress. Alexandra radiated happiness and Nicholas, dressed in the uniform of a Hussar, received the hearty congratulations of his numerous royal cousins. George, Duke of York, and later George V of England, wrote to his wife Mary of Teck, 'I think Nicky is a very lucky man to have got such a lovely and charming wife and I must say I never saw two people more in love with each other or happier than they are.'

Mourning decreed that there should be neither reception nor honeymoon but their marriage began, as it continued, outwardly serene but based on an intense passion. On the morning after her wedding night Alexandra wrote in her husband's diary, 'Never did I believe there could be such utter happiness in this world, such a feeling of unity between two mortal beings. I love you, those three words have my life in them.' In November 1895 Alexandra gave birth to her first child — the Grand Duchess Olga Nicolaievna.

Funeral of Alexander III — the body of the late Tsar lying in state in the Cathedral of St Peter and St Paul, St Petersburg. The mourners are, *from left to right,* the Tsarina (Marie), the Princess of Wales, the Tsar (Nicholas), the Prince of Wales (the future Edward VII), Grand Duke Michael, the Duchess of Coburg, Grand Duke Vladimir, Grand Duke Serge, Princess Alix of Hesse (Alexandra).

3 The new Tsar

As Tsar, newly crowned Nicholas' first task was to tour Europe, making state visits and private courtesy calls to his fellow sovereigns. In the summer of 1896 he saw the ageing Emperor of Austria-Hungary Franz Joseph, the German Kaiser William, his grandparents King Christian IX and Queen Louise of Denmark, Queen Victoria, and lastly, the President of France. The French visit was the climax of the tour and made a deep and lasting impression on Nicholas.

A German cartoonist's view of Nicholas' foreign policy c1895. Germany had not yet reconciled herself to the permanence of the Franco-Russian entente and believed Nicholas was angling to renew the old Russo-German alliance of the Dreikaiserbund (3 Emperors League) on more favourable terms. The picture therefore contrasts his personal correspondence with the Kaiser and his lavish distribution of decorations to high-ranking French officers and diplomats. The caption reads:

The Loving Little Father
Yes, one gets this; the other gets that.
Each gets something different
But each gets something.

The growing military and industrial might of the new German Empire had resulted in binding together Europe's greatest Republic and her most autocratic Empire in an alliance of fear. France nursed a desire for revenge for the defeats of 1870—71, when Prussia had stripped her of the rich provinces of Alsace and Lorraine. Russia wanted a counter-weight to the alliance of Germany and Austria-Hungary which hemmed in her western frontier. The bond was strengthened by heavy French investment in Russian railways and Government stocks and by ceremonial visits which created ties of sentiment between the two peoples. In 1891 the French fleet had visited Kronstadt and the Autocrat of all the Russias stood bareheaded while the band played the *Marseillaise,* France's revolutionary anthem. In 1893 the Russian fleet had returned the compliment by visiting Toulon, and in 1894 a formal treaty of alliance had been concluded. The visit of Tsar Nicholas was regarded by the French Government as being of the utmost importance. It being September, the famed chestnut trees of the boulevards were wired with artificial blooms to give Paris the look of spring. The Tsar was welcomed in mid-Channel by the whole French battle fleet, with flags flying and bands playing. Crowds greeted him enthusiastically everywhere and at a huge military review the soldiers spontaneously broke into cheers of *'Vive l'Empereur!'* Nicholas never forgot these exhilarating demonstrations and vowed that in France's hour of need Russia would not be slow to come to her aid.

The Tsar's visit to Paris, 1896 — Nicholas leaving the Russian Church in the Rue Daru, surrounded by officers and diplomats. Regular exchanges of French and Russian officers sealed the links forged by the Tsar's personal tour.

Back to work

At home Nicholas plunged into 'the awful job I have feared all my life,' coping with mountains of paperwork and the ponderous interventions of his by no means respectful uncles. As head of the House of Romanov Nicholas now had the additional duties of overseeing the Imperial estate — farms, vineyards and plantations to the value of 100 million roubles (£20,000,000); jewellery and art treasures worth nearly twice as much; eight palaces with 15,000 servants and officials; five theatres, the Imperial Academy of Arts and the Imperial Ballet and dozens of hospitals, orphanages, schools and institutions. With pensions of 100,000 roubles a year for each Grand Duke and innumerable calls on imperial charity the Tsar frequently ran short of cash before the end of the year, despite having an annual income of 24 million gold roubles. Nicholas faithfully followed his father's example of hard work and simple living, even down to wearing a peasant blouse and breeches. He had no private secretary, preferring to keep his own desk in order and even to seal envelopes himself. Punctilious in details he failed, however, to master one of the basic skills of government: the efficient management of ambitious and able subordinates. Nicholas hated unpleasant disagreements and far too often cut short a potential conflict by dismissing ministers without explanation, a practice which both deprived him of their services and loyalty and added to the number of those who opposed his policies and methods.

A determined defender of autocracy, undiluted by parliaments or constitutions, Nicholas soon dashed liberal hopes of reform. In this he followed his father, and in foreign affairs too, he wished to continue the pacific policy bequeathed to him. To the amazement of his fellow sovereigns, and to the outright disgust of the Kaiser, Nicholas, commander of the largest army in the world, proposed a Disarmament Conference and the creation of an international tribunal for the peaceful settlement of disputes between states. Even the Prince of Wales dismissed this appeal as 'the greatest nonsense and rubbish I ever heard of'. Nevertheless Nicholas persevered and in May 1899 representatives of twenty powers met at The Hague to discuss the Russian proposals. The policy of disarmament was stifled at birth but the efforts of the Tsar were rewarded by the establishment of rules of warfare and a Permanent Court of Arbitration, the ancestor of today's International Court of Justice. Although Nicholas intended to follow the example of his 'unforgettable' dead father, the Tsar he most admired was not Peter the Great but Alexis the Mild, and already some admiring contemporaries had dubbed him 'Nicholas the Pacific'.

Nicholas and Alexandra — English and Russian; prisoners of the past in the present.

First lady of the Empire

While Nicholas was successfully learning how to rule, Alexandra was struggling to become first lady of the Empire, a role for which her strict German-English upbringing had not been an appropriate training. She was positively shocked by the frivolousness

of St Petersburg, its scandals and gossip and open love affairs. Shyness and nervousness overcame her on formal occasions and she retreated into a cold aloofness; her zeal for her new religion was positively embarrassing. Summoned to the throne from obscurity she had no time to win friends who could help or advise her. The Dowager Empress Marie jealously resented her influence over the Tsar and the death of Queen Victoria (in 1901) deprived her of the one woman in whom she had been able to confide. Her Russian was awkward, her knowledge of court protocol imperfect. She made mistakes — and more important, she unwittingly made enemies. Recurrent pregnancies confined her to seclusion, but failed to produce an heir for Nicholas, as Grand Duchess Olga was succeeded by Tatiana, Marie and Anastasia. Isolated from the aristocracy by her personality and her circumstances Alexandra began to dwell in a private world of her own, peopled by her beloved family and the loyal peasantry, the 'real' Russians to whom she was *Matiushka,* the Little Mother. Difficult ministers, striking workers, revolutionary students intruded, rude and unwelcome, into the fairyland of the Royal Palace. Unable to understand them she either ignored them or pressed Nicholas to be firm and forceful.

Nicky and Willy

Nicholas, labouring under the shadow of his dead father, subject to the exhortations of his uncles, his ministers and his wife, was also pressed from another quarter — the Kaiser. William II was nine years his senior and had been reigning six years longer. Age and experience were on his side and to these advantages he added a swaggering confidence and a determination to bend the youthful, modest Nicholas to his own purposes. Addressing himself to 'Dearest Nicky' signing himself 'your affectionate Willy', the Kaiser deluged Nicholas with flattery and advice. He kept a confidential attaché in the Tsar's private retinue 'to quickly communicate with me . . . without the lumbering and indiscreet apparatus of Chancelleries, Embassies, etc.' He urged Nicholas to be firm in upholding his autocratic rights and to remain on his guard against his republican ally. 'Nicky, take my word, the curse of God has stricken that people for ever. We Christian Kings have one holy duty imposed on us by Heaven: to uphold the principle of the Divine Right of Kings.' Unable to foist this appeal onto the loyal Nicholas, William tried another tack and in this he was successful. He hated Orientals and frequently railed against 'The Yellow Peril' which he believed threatened the supremacy of the West. The alliance of Britain and Japan did nothing to endear either to him, and he urged Nicholas to strike in the East and forestall both these powers from carving up China. Exultantly he urged Russia to undertake this 'Holy Mission.' 'Clearly,' he urged the Tsar, 'it is the great task of the future for Russia to cultivate the Asian continent and to defend Europe from the inroads of the Great Yellow Race. In this you will always find me on your side, ready to help you as best I can . . .'

From Germany's point of view an eastern adventure for the Russians could only be advantageous — it would distract Russia from the Balkans, where Germany's ally Austria could exploit the weakness of the Ottoman Empire and curb the nationalist ambitions of Russia's Slav protégé, Serbia; it would isolate France, Germany's chief rival; and it would almost certainly lead Russia into conflict with either Britain in India or Japan in the Pacific, thus distracting Germany's other rivals and perhaps forcing Russia back to her side.

In 1895 Japan had attacked several territories of the decrepit Chinese Empire. Among these was the ice-free port and fortress of Port Arthur, which Russia had long coveted. Russia intervened and Japan, unwilling to risk a war, was forced to give up the port, which the Russians extracted from the helpless Chinese on a long lease three years later. The occupation of Port Arthur was heady news in St Petersburg. A new spur of the Trans-Siberian Railway was constructed, offering a new link to the East. During the disturbances of the Boxer rising of 1900, the Russians had taken the opportunity of occupying Manchuria. All that remained, the Tsar's military advisers urged him, was the seizure of Korea itself. Already a group of Russian adventurers had formed the Yalu Timber Company and had began to infiltrate Russian soldiers into Korea in the guise of workmen. War itself would be a mere formality and would also distract the Russian people from demands for social reform. Confidently Russia snubbed Japanese attempts to reach a peaceful settlement and sent Marquis Ito away empty-handed.

The Russo-Japanese War

In the event, the decision was taken out of the Tsar's hands. On the evening of February 6th, 1904, Nicholas returned from the theatre to be handed a telegram from Admiral Alexeiev, Russian Viceroy and Commander-in-Chief in the Far East.

A Japanese view of the surprise attack on Port Arthur.

'About midnight, Japanese destroyers made a sudden attack on the squadron anchored in the outer harbour of Port Arthur. The battleships *Tsarevich, Retvizan* and the cruiser *Pallada* were torpedoed. The importance of the damage is being ascertained.'

Nicholas was stunned by the tragedy at Port Arthur, but the enthusiasm and patriotic loyalty of his people cheered him for the coming struggle. In the event it was an unmitigated disaster for Russia. Operating only a few hundred miles by sea from their base of supplies, the Japanese were soon

able to land 150,000 men, overwhelming local Russian forces and laying siege to Port Arthur, the main Russian base. The Tsar's Army, 3 million strong, was almost powerless to intervene, for the 4,000-mile Trans-Siberian Railway was single track for much of its length and, having been hastily constructed, was unable to bear the weight of continuous supply trains. At the mountainous southern end of Lake Baikal there was, moreover, a gap of 100 miles, bridged in summer by ferries, in winter by sledges drawn across the ice.

Heroism and gallantry were common to

both sides but Japan, having seized the initiative, had secured command of the seas and hemmed in the Russian fleet with minefields. On April 13th the battleship *Petropavlovsk* ventured out of Port Arthur, struck a mine and sank with the loss of 700 men and the brilliant Admiral Makarov. Soon after this loss, Russia was forced to recognize how thoroughly Japan had leaped from feudalism to modern industrial and military power. Military instructors from France and Germany, and naval advisers from England had helped Japan turn her new industrial power into the base for a superb Army and Navy. Inexorably, though at great cost, Japan edged towards total victory.

In January 1905 Port Arthur surrendered. It had cost Russia 28,000 men, Japan more than twice as many. Around Mukden the two armies clashed in the mightiest battle yet fought, involving three-quarters of a million men. After three days of bloody fighting with 50,000 casualties on each side, the Russians were forced to withdraw. A last desperate gamble remained. In October 1904 the Russian Baltic Fleet, strengthened by a ramshackle assemblage of transports and training ships, had set sail for Japan, intending to restore Russian naval supremacy. On May 27th, 1905 the exhausted expedition, having steamed halfway round the world, appeared in the Strait of Tsushima, 7,000 yards from the waiting guns of Admiral Togo and the Japanese Navy. The greatest sea battle since Trafalgar lasted less than an hour. Ripped

apart by the accuracy of the Japanese gunnery, crippled by high-speed torpedo boats, the Russian fleet lost eight battle-ships, seven cruisers and six destroyers. A pitiful remnant limped away, to be interned or destroyed by the Japanese at their leisure.

Prompted by the Japanese, whose very success had temporarily exhausted their reserves of men, money and supplies, President Theodore Roosevelt of the

United States offered to mediate between the two powers. Russia gratefully accepted the offer and Sergius Witte was dispatched to negotiate the terms of a definitive Treaty at Portsmouth, New Hampshire. Witte's charm and skilful cultivation of the Press won considerable sympathy for the Russian cause and the Japanese, out-manoeuvred by the brilliant Russian, were unable to exploit their military victory to the full.

Witte (right) in thoughtful pose at Portsmouth, New Hampshire. With him is Baron von Rosen, the other Russian plenipotentiary.

4 1905

Witte's diplomatic success was, however, little consolation to the Tsar, who was now grappling with a grave internal crisis. The humiliating surrender of Port Arthur had touched off a wave of protest against the mismanagement of the war. Patriotic sentiments, frustrated and angered by Japanese victories, turned into a swelling chorus of discontent. Strikes, meetings and demonstrations led to demands for reform, and the popular movement thrust to the fore a young St Petersburg priest, Father George Gapon. Gapon led a movement secretly created and guided by the police. The Assembly of Russian Workingmen aimed to immunize the workers against the plague of Socialism and strengthen their attachment to Orthodoxy and the Tsar. Sincere in his beliefs and carried away by the extravagance of his own speeches and the fervour of his eager audiences, Gapon abandoned his role as police agent for that of popular leader and started a mass movement to petition the Tsar for reform. Denouncing 'despotic and irresponsible government,' the petition attacked the 'capitalistic exploiters, crooks and robbers of the Russian people' and appealed to the Tsar to grant his people a parliament, the vote, universal education, a minimum wage, an eight-hour day, an income tax, separation of church and state, and amnesty for all political prisoners.

Bloody Sunday

On Sunday morning, January 22nd, 1905, Gapon led his march to present the petition. Nicholas, secluded in the royal estate at Tsarskoe Selo, fifteen miles from St Petersburg, had known nothing of either march or petition until the previous evening. Confident that Mirsky, the newly appointed liberal Minister of the Interior had the situation well in hand, he passed a peaceful weekend with his family. In St Petersburg meanwhile, massive crowds, arms linked, converged on the Winter Palace through the icy streets, bearing icons and singing the Imperial anthem 'God Save the Tsar.' Uncertain in the face of such masses, isolated units of Cossacks and Hussars began to open fire on the crowds. The official figures announced ninety-two dead and hundreds wounded. The actual number was probably higher but rumour exaggerated the number tenfold or more. The futile, useless massacre of 'Bloody Sunday' struck deep at the bond of trust between Tsar and people and the legend of 'Bloody Nicholas' was born.

Only the beginning...

'Bloody Sunday' was only the beginning of a year of terror. In February Grand Duke Serge, uncle to the Tsar and husband of Ella, Alexandra's elder sister, was blown apart by an assassin's bomb. As the months rolled by, violence spread to every corner of Russia. Nicholas, distracted by the war, was perturbed by the indecisiveness of his ministers. 'It makes me sick to read the news,' he wrote,'strikes in schools and factories, murdered policemen, Cossacks, riots. But the ministers, instead of acting

with quick decision, only assemble in council like a lot of frightened hens and cackle about providing united ministerial action.'

When the news of the disaster at Tsushima came through, the crew of the battleship *Potemkin* threw their officers overboard, raised the red flag of revolution and steamed along the Black Sea coast, bombarding towns until the need for fuel forced them to intern at the Rumanian port of Constanza. In mid-October the whole nation was paralysed by a general strike, which stopped trains, ships, factories, schools and hospitals from Warsaw to the Urals. Newspapers failed to appear, electric lights flickered out, street corner revolutionaries inflamed the chanting crowds who thronged the streets. Red flags flew from the rooftops of the cities and in the countryside the peasants, worn down by poverty, famine, taxation and conscription, pillaged the houses and barns of the landowners.

Peasant risings were familiar enough; what was novel and terrifying was the new form of workers' organization — the Soviet, a council of elected delegates, each delegate respresenting 1,000 workers. Inspired by the fiery oratory of Leon Trotsky, a member of the forbidden Marxist Social Democratic Party, the Soviets threatened to wreck the factories and turn a general strike into a full scale revolution. In this crisis Nicholas summoned to his aid Sergius Witte, fresh

Police and Cossacks disperse a peaceful crowd of demonstrators 1905.

from his success at the Portsmouth peace conference.

Witte

Sergius Witte was a huge, burly man and the ablest administrator in the Tsar's service. Of Dutch descent he had worked his way up from humble beginnings. At the University of Odessa he showed outstanding talent in mathematics. During Russia's war against Turkey in 1877 he distinguished himself in the complex task of supervising the transport of men and supplies to the front. In 1892 as Minister of Communications he energetically promoted the construction of the Trans-Siberian Railway; elevated to the key post of Minister of Finance he tripled Russia's industrial output. His ingenious brain brought the Russian currency onto the sure base of the gold standard and by his creation of a state vodka monopoly he brought millions into the Imperial treasury each year. Cynical and arrogant, Witte's genius earned the grudging admiration, even of his political enemies.

Sergius Witte, who gave Russia its first constitution and parliament, believed in neither. In a famous letter to his mother Nicholas described Witte's policy:

'We very often met in the early morning to part only in the evening when night fell. There were only two ways open: to find an

Street-fighting 1905 — barricades were erected to obstruct the movement of troops and seal off strategic points.

energetic soldier to crush the rebellion by sheer force. There would be time to breathe then but, as likely as not, one would have to use force again in a few months, and that would mean rivers of blood and in the end we should be where we started.

'The other way out would be to give the people their civil rights, freedom of speech and Press, also to have all laws confirmed by a state Duma or parliament — that of course would be a constitution. Witte defends this energetically. He says that, while it is not without risk, it is the only way out at the present moment. Almost everybody I had an opportunity of consulting is of the same opinion . . . He . . . drew up a Manifesto. We discussed it for two days and in the end, invoking God's help, I signed it . . . My only consolation is that such is the will of God and this grave decision will lead my dear Russia out of the intolerable chaos she has been in for nearly a year.'

The Imperial Manifesto of October 30th, 1905, gave Russia a Duma, and her people civil rights. The Tsar retained sole control of defence and foreign affairs and the undisputed power to appoint and dismiss ministers. In parts of the nation the Manifesto, by stripping local police of many of their powers, led directly to violence. In the Baltic states peasant risings against German landlords gave birth to a rash of village republics; in the Ukraine, Kiev and Odessa there were right-wing pogroms against the Jews, the traditional scapegoats for Russia's ills; in the Trans-

Caucasus the Armenians suffered at the hands of hysterical mobs; Poland and Finland, subject territories for nearly a century, clamoured for independence; at Kronstadt and Sevastopol there were naval mutinies; and in December the Moscow Soviet called out 2,000 workers and students to the barricades, proclaiming a Provisional Government which held off Imperial forces for ten days until the Semenovsky Regiment of the Guard cleared the streets with artillery and bayonets. Baffled and dejected Nicholas dismissed Witte on the eve of the Duma's first meeting.

Confrontation 1905 — defiant weavers refuse to compromise their support for the general strike.

5

An heir to the throne

In the midst of war and the threat of revolution Nicholas was learning to bear a new and secret affliction. On August 12th, 1904, he had joyfully recorded in his diary — 'A great never-to-be-forgotten day when the mercy of God has visited us so clearly. Alix gave birth to a son at one o'clock. The child has been called Alexis.' The eight-pound baby, the first male heir to be born to a reigning Russian Tsar since the 17th century, was saluted by 301 guns. His birth was greeted as an omen of hope in a time of trouble. It was not to be. Born in the shadow of war and revolution Alexis was cursed with haemophilia, the blood disease which gave the wretched child a brief lifetime of pain and brought his parents, through fear and anguish, to a premature old age. Along with his father's well-intentioned blundering, Russia's breakneck economic development and the strains imposed by strikes, famines and disastrous war, the dreadful secret of the heir to the throne helped to topple the most powerful dynasty in the world.

Tsarskoe Selo

In Tsarskoe Selo, 'the Tsar's village' the secret of Alexis' disease could be kept hidden from the world, from diplomats who might fear for the security of a dynasty whose survival would depend on a semi-invalid, from revolutionary assassins who might be tempted by such a vulnerable target. In the Tsarskoe Selo Alexis and his secret were safe.

Surrounded by a high iron fence, guarded by ceaseless patrols of scarlet-clad Cossacks and 5,000 infantry, the Imperial Park was like an enchanted fairyland to the few outsiders privileged to see it — 800 acres of smooth lawns set with arches, monuments, fountains and pagodas; an artificial lake, big enough for a sailing boat but capable of being emptied and refilled like a huge bath tub; and two residences, the Catherine Palace with 200 rooms and the Alexander Palace with 100 rooms. Here the Imperial family spent the winter, the children at their lessons, Nicholas at his paperwork or taking exercise out of doors.

In March they departed for the flowering gardens of the Crimea; in May they moved to a villa on the Baltic coast at Peterhof; in June they cruised the Finnish fjords aboard the Imperial yacht, *Standart;* in August they visited the Polish forests to hunt; in September the Crimea once more and then in November back to Tsarskoe Selo where they would spend the winter. Surrounded by their favourite servants, books and furniture the Imperial family was cushioned by protocol and unvarying routine from contact with a Russia they knew only from the windows of the Imperial train and the carefully phrased reports of ministers chosen by His Imperial Majesty.

Haemophilia

'Alexis was the centre of this united family,' wrote Pierre Gilliard, his tutor. 'His sisters worshipped him. He was his parents' pride and joy. When he was well, the palace was transformed. Everyone and everything in it seemed bathed in sun-

shine.' He was a handsome, lively child, intelligent and full of curiosity. For months he could live a normal life and then a minor accident could bring a major crisis for the whole family. A bump or fall which ruptured a blood vessel would start an internal flow of blood which, refusing to clot, would run unchecked for hours, until the skin swelled out in bumps the size of a grapefruit and the very pressure of the swelling slowed down the haemorrhage until a clot finally formed and the slow process of re-absorption took place. Bleeding into the joints meant pressure on the nerves, agonizing pain and paralysis. Morphine, though available, was denied the Tsarevich for fear of addiction. Instead he was condemned to faint from pain as his agonized parents watched helplessly at his bedside, knowing that even if the crisis passed successfully he might be crippled for weeks or even months afterwards, forced to endure constant hot mud baths and heavy iron orthopaedic devices to straighten his crooked limbs.

Watched over day and night by his sailor bodyguards, Derevenko and Nagorny, Alexis played with hundreds of elaborate

A German cartoon of the 1905 revolution. Nicholas II, nursing his infant son, is surrounded by a sea of rebellion. The waves are labelled Moscow, Kronstadt, Lodz, Warsaw, Odessa. The lightning spells out — Tsushima. The caption reads:—

The waves sweep high and low,
The breakers strike here and there,
And the old man sits on the roof,
Not knowing how to help himself.

mechanical toys but was denied a bicycle and forbidden to play tennis or run about barefoot. His many pets amused him and he learned to play the balalaika well, but his passion was for military reviews, though he soon realized he could never be the soldier-Tsar of his dreams.

His mother, isolated, nervous, blaming herself for transmitting the disease, lived a life of constant tension. A severe bout of bleeding for Alexis meant constant attendance at his side, sleepless nights and fearful days as the doctors and specialists struggled to stem the flow of blood. When the crisis passed, physically exhausted and emotionally drained, she would take to her bed for weeks, knowing that she must regain her strength to help her son face the next crisis that was certain to come, though none could know when or predict whether or not it would prove fatal. Constant anxiety, following on five difficult pregnancies took toll of her health. She spent most mornings in bed, avoided social occasions and was unable to attend public or cermonial functions. The secret of her son's disease was known only to a few; Gilliard, Alexis' tutor from 1912, had taught his sisters for eight years without ever learning why the little Tsarevich was sometimes confined to his bed for weeks at a time. What St Petersburg did not know it was ready to invent and alarming rumours were accepted as explanations of the curious imperfections in the Imperial

The infant Alexis, an official portrait by the court photographer. Ominously the English caption reads:— 'The photograph itself is sufficient proof of how admirably the Tsarevich has thriven in adversity, although this week there was a rumour that he was seriously ill.' The picture was taken, in March 1906, at the express wish of the Empress who was determined to present her son to the world as a normal, healthy boy.

Aboard the Standart — in the background a naval escort, in the foreground Alexis acts as guard of honour to his father.

family's facade of normalcy. Some said
Alexis was an epileptic, others that he was
mentally retarded. Alexandra likewise
suffered from these stories. Never as
popular as she had wished to be in her
youth, she became even less popular.
Unaware of her ordeal to keep her son
alive, Russia regarded her seclusion as
proof of her distaste and contempt for the
people whose loyalty she in fact desper-
ately longed for.

Alexis, in a sailor suit, accompanied by the
'faithful' Derevenko, who bullied and then
abandoned his small master when the
Revolution broke out. The photograph was
taken shortly after a hair's breadth escape
near the Castle of Livonia when a foreign
visitor's car knocked both Derevenko and
Alexis off their bicycles.

6 Stolypin

The dismissal of Witte obliged Nicholas to search for a new Chief Minister. He found him in Peter Arkadyevich Stolypin, a bluff, hearty member of the Russian rural gentry, the class which provided the Tsar with his local officials and most loyal supporters but few candidates for high office, which was generally the prerogative of the princely aristocracy or career bureaucrats. Stolypin was a passionate monarchist, and patriot, an eloquent speaker and an energetic administrator. In the Duma he glowered at the representatives of the Left and warned them 'You want great upheavals, but we want a great Russia.'

He had made his mark as governor of Saratov province, an area which saw some of the most violent upheavals in 1905, but which he suppressed with minimal loss of life by fearlessly approaching groups of rebels alone and persuading them to lay down their arms. Created Minister of Interior early in 1906 he soon replaced the aged Goremykin as the Tsar's right hand. He took a firm line against the few remaining insurgents and within a month his house was the target for an assassin's bomb which

Royal sailors at Cowes — Nicholas (right) with Alexis, the Prince of Wales (the future George V) and his son (the future Edward VIII, now Duke of Windsor, the Tsar's godson).

killed thirty-two people and maimed two of his children but left him unscathed.

Land reforms

Stolypin's strategy was to suppress violence and simultaneously introduce reforms which would end all reasonable grievances. His most important measure was a new land law which enabled peasants to exchange the strips of land they held in the communal fields for compact blocks which could be more efficiently farmed and bequeathed to their sons. In this way Stolypin aimed to create a large class of small landowners with a vested interest in the stability of the Government. Nicholas gave the plan his personal support and four million acres of Crown lands were sold to the Government for re-sale on easy terms to the peasants. By 1914, 9 million peasant families owned their own farms.

Even Nature seemed to smile on Stolypin's efforts. The years 1906-11 were years of good weather and good harvests with the best crops in living memory. Food was plentiful, taxes were paid promptly and the Government even managed to show a surplus. Encouraged by the prosperity of agriculture and the sound management of Government revenues foreign investment poured in to finance the construction of more railways and help coal and iron mines break new records for production. A spate of reformist legislation was passed by the Duma — the principle of free primary school education was established and Press censorship abolished. Stolypin seemed to have upstaged even the most ardent reformers and by changing the electoral laws to concentrate voting power in the hands of the country gentry, had brought the Duma to heel and given it a useful part to play in assisting the Government. Even Nicholas began to have confidence in it. The memories of the Duma's first two stormy sessions began to fade and moderate liberals looked forward with confidence to the gradual emergence of a western-style parliamentary form of government.

Stolypin, having done so much to secure the throne from the threat of revolution, did not live to see the fruition of his work. In September 1911, at the Kiev Opera House and in the presence of the Tsar, he was shot twice in the chest at point blank range by the police agent assigned to protect him. Stolypin died five days later. When it became known that his assassin, the secret revolutionary Mordka Bogrov, was a Jew, the Orthodox population of Kiev prepared for a pogrom while the Jewish community besieged the railway station in their desperation to escape. Kokovtsov, the Finance Minister, on his own initiative ordered three regiments of Cossacks into the city to prevent violence and telegraphed the governors of the region to take appropriate precautions. Nicholas confirmed these wise measures and named him as Stolypin's successor. No sooner had he settled in office than the Tsar's new Chief Minister found himself faced with a political situation of the utmost delicacy and importance — the question of Rasputin.

The other cousin — Nicholas and Kaiser William (with cigar) set out for a day's hunting (1910).

Rasputin

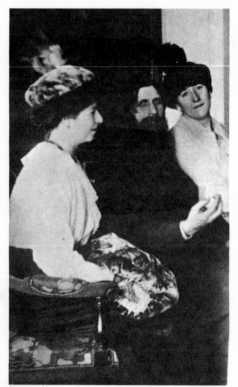

Rasputin in characteristic pose.

Rasputin was born in 1872, his name Gregory Efimovich, his home Pokrovskoe on the Tura River in Western Siberia. He grew up an aggressive, drunken and eloquent rake. Earning his living as a waggoner he chanced to carry a traveller to the monastery of Verkhoturye; while there he learned that it was the prison of a number of members of the Khlysty, an heretical sect which believed in reaching God through the sexual ecstasies of nocturnal orgies. Fascinated, Rasputin remained there for four months, closely observing both the monks and their captives.

Returning to Pokrovskoe Rasputin, now twenty, married a blonde peasant girl and took up farming. Declaring one day that a vision had directed him to undertake a pilgrimage he abandoned his wife, two daughters and mentally deficient son, and walked 2,000 miles to the monastery of Mount Athos in Greece. When he returned two years later he came as a new man, praying for the sick, abstaining from drink. The village priest, alarmed at his growing influence, threatened to charge him with heresy. Rasputin, therefore, left his home

and began to wander again, arriving in St Petersburg, where he was honourably received by the saintly Father John of Kronstadt in 1903. Two years later he returned, a gifted preacher reputed to possess extraordinary powers. Grand Duchess Militsa, a Montenegrin princess with a taste for the occult, introduced him to Tsarskoe Selo, where he became a regular visitor. The Imperial couple were charmed by his simple, respectful peasant manner and his language, full of quotations from the Bible and old Russian proverbs. The infant Alexis was enthralled by his tales of Siberia and soon he came to hold an almost hypnotic fascination for all the Grand Duchesses as well.

'Holy' or 'Dissolute'?

Received by the Tsar himself, Rasputin soon gathered a large band of devoted followers, convinced of his holiness, or at least titillated by his repulsive manners, dirty beard and vile body odour. Sophisticated women regarded him as an exotic

Das neue Wappen.

Trier

Die Schnäbel hacken mit Gewalt;
So sollen sie's nur weitertreiben,

Dann wird vom Russenadler bald
Ein schöner Vogel übrig bleiben!

diversion and clamoured for his rough caresses. Eagerly Rasputin responded and exploited, but took care never to drop his facade with the Imperial family or with Alexandra's plain, devoted companion Anna Vyrubova, whose marriage he had prophesied and who regarded him as a genuine *starets*, a Man of God. To her and to Alexandra his nickname 'Rasputin,' 'the dissolute,' was a reference to the past he shunned, not to the present when he was the subject of so many malicious 'lies.'

When Archbishop Theophan, respected Inspector of the Theological Academy and former confessor to the Empress, began to express doubts about Rasputin he was exiled to the Bishopric of the Crimea. When Iliodor, the fanatical young monk who had at first worshipped Rasputin, turned against him after he had heard that his master had attempted to rape a nun, Iliodor was unfrocked. Alexandra refused to hear ill of Rasputin. 'They accuse Rasputin of kissing women,' she wrote to Nicholas. 'Read the Apostles; they kissed everybody as a form of greeting.' By 1912 she was ready to defend him against the world — because she believed he could keep Alexis alive.

By 1912 Rasputin's reputation had

The New Crest. A satirical cartoon reveals the German reaction to Russia's internal troubles. The caption reads — 'Let the beaks peck each other until the Russian eagle becomes a nice little bird!' Notice the orb transformed into an anarchist's bomb. The inset shield shows a Russian soldier stabbing the Tsarist dragon.

37

passed beyond the stage of public scandal to become a major political issue in the Duma. The Press, freed from censorship, published the wildest allegations about his activities — the Empress shared his bed, the Grand Duchesses were members of his personal harem, he controlled all major appointments in the Church and Government. Nicholas was furious and demanded that his ministers put an end to the Press campaign; his ministers, however, believed the affair could only be ended by ridding the court of Rasputin, and finally Michael Rodzianko, the President of the Duma and a loyal monarchist, pleaded on his knees with the Tsar that a full investigation be conducted into Rasputin's life and character. Stolypin had tried a similar tactic, but Nicholas had rejected his report. Likewise with Rodzianko he closed his eyes to what he would not and could not believe and while the outcry against Rasputin rose higher and higher the 'Holy Devil' made his place at court more secure than ever.

'The little one will not die'

In the autumn of 1912 the Imperial family travelled to Spala, the ancient hunting lodge of the Kings of Poland. Here the Tsarevich nearly died after a jolting carriage ride gave him a severe internal haemorrhage. Specialists rushed to join his personal physicians but all were powerless to stop the flow of blood into the child's groin and abdomen. A massive external swelling forced his leg up against his chest and he screamed day and night with the pain for eleven days, while his mother sat in anguish by his side. An official announcement of the grave illness of the heir to the throne plunged Russia into prayer as special services were held throughout the Empire, but all hope faded and the suffering boy received the last sacrament while a bulletin was composed

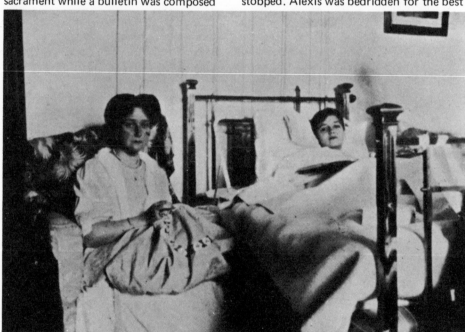

The crisis at Spala 1912 — the Empress, pale and drawn, embroiders at the bedside of Alexis. For 11 days the bleeding continued. Then Rasputin sent a telegram — 'The Little One will not die'.

announcing his death. At this hour, when all hope was gone, Alexandra sent a telegram to Rasputin at his home in Pokrovskoe. He immediately cabled back:

'God has seen your tears and heard your prayers. Do not grieve. The Little One will not die.'

Within thirty-six hours the bleeding stopped. Alexis was bedridden for the best part of a year but his mother was now convinced that his life, and thus the future of the dynasty, lay in Rasputin's hands.

On the brink

The year 1913 marked the tercentenary of the Romanov dynasty, and was suitably celebrated with elaborate pageantry. For the Tsar and his family the demonstrations of public loyalty which spontaneously occurred on their royal progress through the Empire was a convincing reassurance that the throne was still secure in the affections of the people. 'Wherever we went,' wrote Grand Duchess Olga [the Tsar's sister] 'we met with manifestations of loyalty bordering on wildness. When our steamer went down the Volga we saw crowds of peasants wading waist-high in the water to catch a glimpse of Nicky. In some of the towns I would see artisans and workmen falling down to kiss his shadow as we passed.'

This heartening picture was marred by the fact that 700,000 workers were out on strike. By January 1914 the number had grown to a million and bloody fighting between police and workers had broken out in the Baku oil fields.

By mid summer 1914 the number on strike had reached 1½ million and barricades had begun to appear in the streets of St Petersburg. In these chaotic circumstances Count Pourtalès the German Ambassador, confidently assured the Kaiser that Russia could not possibly take up arms if war broke out.

Uniforms of the Imperial Army (left to right) — horseguard, His Majesty's hussar, hussar, Preobrajensky regiment, Cossack bodyguard of his Imperial Majesty.

The assassination

Looking back it is now possible to see the assassination of Arch Duke Franz Ferdinand, the heir to the throne of Austria-Hungary, as the spark which set off the European powderkeg. In retrospect war seems to have been inevitable — powerful empires, backed by conscript armies of millions, locked together by a complex series of alliances, wrangled with each other over colonial possessions or 'spheres of influence' in vital strategic areas like the Middle East or the Balkans. War had seemed imminent on three or four occasions in the decade before 1914 but Franz Ferdinand's death in Sarajevo at the hands of a Serbian terrorist was regarded as a minor, though appalling incident. In London, Paris and Rome shoulders shrugged as if to say that such things were always happening in the Balkans. 'Nothing to cause anxiety,' the French newspaper *Figaro* reassured its readers. 'Terrible shock for the dear old Emperor,' George V wrote in his diary. The Tsar and the Kaiser continued with their usual summer cruises but in Vienna Field Marshal Conrad von Hötzendorf took the first steps which led to war. The assassination was, he argued, 'Serbia's declaration of war on Austria-Hungary;' the perfect pretext for a rapid war of conquest to crush 'the Serbian viper' and secure Austria-Hungary's dominance of the Balkans.

July was a month of feverish diplomatic manoeuvring. Austria-Hungary presented Serbia with a list of humiliating demands amounting almost to annexation and designed to goad Serbia into firing the first shots and appearing the aggressor. Almost thrown off balance by Serbia's decision to accept her demands rather than face annihilation Austria-Hungary determined to press the issue, confident that Russia's internal chaos would prevent her from intervening. The Russian Army was, moreover, known to be in the throes of re-equipping. Within a year or two the process would be complete and there would be no second chance to settle with Serbia. As it was, Germany had given full support to whatever her ally might do; France would never move unless Russia did and England had no interest in the matter. At 5 a.m. on July 29th, a month and a day after the assassination of Franz Ferdinand, Austro-Hungarian artillery began hurling shells across the Danube into Belgrade, the capital of Serbia.

In the event the calculations of the central powers were disastrously wrong. Russia was still smarting from its defeat at the hands of Japan and also determined to avenge Austria-Hungary's annexation of Bosnia-Herzegovina in 1907 when Russia had suffered a traumatic loss of face in diplomatic circles. The Kaiser, realizing too late that the moment of reckoning had come, appealed personally to Nicholas to cancel Russia's mobilization while Germany's mobilization continued. When Nicholas refused, Germany declared war on both Russia and her ally France and started to move on Paris via Belgium, (whose neutrality was guaranteed by a treaty signed by all the great powers in 1839). To Germany's astonishment her violation of Belgian neutrality brought Britain into the war against her. A week after the shelling of Belgrade Europe was divided into two armed camps.

Dancing aboard the royal yacht *Standart* — Grand Duchess Tatiana and Grand Duchess Olga flirt with Russian officers.

9 The summer of 1914

In Russia the announcement of the outbreak of war was greeted with an upsurge of patriotic fervour. Massive crowds gathered before the Winter Palace to sing the Imperial anthem. The war was popularly regarded as a Holy Crusade against the Germans and Nicholas reinforced this impression by changing the name of the capital from the German 'St Petersburg' to the Slav 'Petrograd.' Two men were not carried away by war fever — Rasputin and Witte. Witte bluntly told the French ambassador Paléologue that from Russia's point of view the war was madness, Slav solidarity was simply nonsense and Russia could hope for nothing from the war — the Empire was so vast already that no territory could be worth fighting for or compensate her for the millions of men who would inevitably be killed. Defeat for Germany and Austria-Hungary would simply mean their replacement by a rash of republics who would inevitably infect Russia with the disease of revolution.

The first of the many — Russian soldiers march off to Petrograd railway station to travel to the front.

Rasputin offered none of Witte's close-reasoned arguments. Instead he sent a brief and ominous telegram to the Tsar, the Little Father — 'Let Papa not plan war, for with the war will come the end of Russia and yourselves and you will lose to the last man.'

The Russian steamroller

Russia and her allies placed their faith in her Army, the famous 'Russian steamroller.' Its pre-war regular strength was 1,400,000; mobilization added 3,100,000 reserves and millions more stood ready behind them. In every other respect, however, Russia was unprepared for war.
'The Russian steam-roller' — a bayonet-charge in best textbook style.

Germany had ten times as much railway track per square mile and whereas Russian soldiers travelled an average of 800 miles to reach the front, German soldiers travelled less than a quarter of that distance. Russian heavy industry was still too small to equip the massive armies the Tsar could raise and her reserves of munitions were pitifully small. With the Baltic barred by German U-boats and the Dardanelles by the guns of her former ally Turkey, Russia could receive help from her allies only via Archangel which was frozen solid in winter, or Vladivostock, which was over 4,000 miles from the front line. The Russian High Command was moreover gravely weakened by the mutual contempt of Sukhomlinov, the fawning and ineffectual Minister of War and Grand Duke Nicolaievich, the redoubtable warrior giant who commanded the armies in the field.

The Germans, aware of Russia's weaknesses and their own superiority in both transport capacity and fire-power, had evolved a plan which they believed would enable them to beat both France and Russia. Outlined by the brilliant General Schlieffen in the 1890s, when the Franco-Russian alliance had first confronted Germany with the nightmare of a war on two fronts, the plan was elaborated over the succeeding twenty years into a meticulous timetable in which every soldier, every railway-wagon, every shell, had its appointed part to play. In essence the Schlieffen plan was simple: drive through Belgium and Northern France to Paris while holding the partially mobilized Russians in the East. In six weeks Paris would have been taken and then the full might of the German Army could be turned eastwards before the Russians had completed their ponderous mobilization. Then, with the aid of Austria-Hungary, the

invasion of Russia could begin. The Kaiser characteristically put it even more bluntly — 'Lunch in Paris, dinner in St Petersburg.'

The French, though ignorant of the details of the Schlieffen plan, were aware

'For the greater glory of the Empire' — a patriotic postcard featuring Nicholas as the hero of Russia's entry into the war.

that Russia's strength must be brought to bear as quickly as possible on the German rear. For this reason the massive loans which she had made to her ally were given strictly on condition that railways be built leading to the German frontier. When hostilities began, her worst fears were confirmed. By September 2nd, less than a

month after crossing the frontier, the advance guard of the Kaiser's Army was within thirty miles of Paris.

In response to the desperate pleas of her ally Russia, half prepared, had lumbered into a two-pronged attack. General Rennenkampf's First Army of 200,000 advanced south-west, parallel to the Baltic

Царствуй на страхъ врагамъ

coast, into East Prussia, and, on August 20th partially defeated the German covering forces allotted to delay their advance. Inexplicably, Rennenkampf halted after his victory while General Samsonov's Second Army of 170,000 toiled northwards from Poland. The desperate German General Staff, anxious that no complication delay the timetable of their advance in the west, dispatched two aged generals to patch up the situation as best they could and on August

highest stakes. Leaving only two brigades of cavalry to face the still motionless Rennenkampf they bundled every available German soldier south to confront Samsonov. Surrounded on three sides, pounded by vastly superior artillery, Samsonov's Second Army disintegrated in four days of bloody fighting. Russian losses amounted to 110,000 men, including 90,000 prisoners. Samsonov shot himself, and the Germans named their victory the

dissatisfied with the battle. Their advance had caused the Germans to panic and recall two Army corps and a cavalry division from their right wing in France. They arrived too late to affect the outcome at Tannenberg, but they could not be returned in time to turn the balance against the French and British at the Marne. The sacrifice of Tannenberg, willingly made, saved Paris, but by the end of 1914, after only five months of war, 1 million

Guarding the regimental colours. The motto — 'God is with us'.

23rd, Paul Hindenburg and Erich Ludendorff arrived to take command in the East.

Their strategy was a gamble for the

Dug-out trenches on the Eastern Front.
Battle of Tannenberg, in revenge for a famous Slav victory over the Teutonic Knights near the same place in 1410.

Although Rennenkampf was relieved of command, the Russians were by no means

Russians, a quarter of the Army, had been killed, wounded or taken prisoner.

10 Nicholas takes command

In March, 1915 the Russian Army, swollen by 2 million new recruits, hurled itself against the Austrians in Galicia, taking Przemysl, the strongest fortress in the Hapsburg Empire with 120,000 prisoners and 900 guns. Gallantly the Russians pushed on through the Carpathians in the teeth of a desperate defence by crack Hungarian regiments. Convinced that Austria-Hungary was about to disintegrate Italy, previously neutral, joined the Allies against the Central Powers.

Germany, meanwhile, was preparing with quiet efficiency to aid her ally. On May 2nd, 1,500 guns opened fire on a single sector of the Russian line in Southern Poland. Seven hundred thousand shells rained down during the four-hour barrage and the Russian division which lay immediately in its path was reduced from 16,000 men to 500. The Third Caucasian Corps, rushed in to fill the breach, was quickly reduced from 40,000 men to 6,000, though even that remnant contrived to attack by night with bayonets and take 7,000 prisoners. In May and June the Russian Third Army, which took the brunt

The steam-roller in reverse. The Russian army in full retreat.

of the German bombardment, reeled under the blows inflicted upon it and a general withdrawal began. General Belaiev reported to Nicholas from Stavka, the Russian field headquarters, that, 'In recent battles a third of the men had no rifles. These poor devils had to wait patiently until their comrades fell before their eyes and they could pick up weapons. The Army is drowning in its own blood.'

Heavy losses breed disorder at home

General Deniken, retreating from Galicia, wrote: 'The German heavy artillery swept away whole lines of trenches, and their defenders with them. We hardly replied — there was nothing with which we could reply. Our regiments, although completely

'*Kamerad!*' Russian troops surrender.

exhausted, were beating off one attack after another by bayonet . . . Blood flowed unendingly, the ranks became thinner and thinner. The number of graves constantly multiplied.' Total losses for the spring and summer of 1915 amounted to 1,400,000 killed or wounded, while 976,000 had been taken prisoner. On August 5th, with the Army in retreat, Warsaw fell. Defeat at the front bred disorder at home. At first the targets were German and for three days in June shops, bakeries, factories, private houses and country estates belonging to people with German names were looted and burned. Then the inflamed mob turned on the Government — the Empress should be shut up in a convent, the Tsar deposed and Rasputin hanged. Nicholas was by no means deaf to these discontents. An emergency session of the Duma was summoned and a

The Little Father takes command.

Special Defence Council established, its members drawn from both Duma representatives and the Tsar's appointed ministers. The energetic and efficient General Polivanov replaced Sukhomlinov as Minister of War. But the retreat continued and Nicholas, urged on by Alexandra against the united advice of his ministers, made a momentous decision — to relieve Grand Duke Nicholas and take personal command of the armies in the field.

France and England regarded the Tsar's gesture as a firm pledge of his determination not to make a separate peace. The German Field Marshall, Ludendorff, even with his own Army in full advance, was pleased to see the departure of Grand Duke Nicholas, whom he regarded as 'a great soldier and strategist.' The Tsar, he knew, would only be a figurehead. The real command would fall on his Chief of Staff, Alexeiev, an able and dynamic general whose major failing was a desire to do everything himself.

The Russians, now fighting on their own soil, began to contest every foot of ground they yielded. By November the 200-mile German advance had been halted. Through the winter the Army could recuperate for the next trial of strength. In 1916, to distract the Germans from their concentrated assault on the French fortress of Verdun the Russian Army would advance once more, and would lose 1,200,000 men.

But the military collapse of 1915 had consequences far beyond the strategy of battle. The Tsar's decision to take personal command of the Army meant, in effect, his abdication from all but a vague, supervisory control over affairs of state. In an autocracy this arrangement was unworkable; a substitute autocrat had to take his place in practice. Uncertainly at first, then with growing confidence, Empress Alexandra came to assume this role, at her side, her trusted friend and counsellor — Rasputin.

11 The Government disintegrates

Alexandra had, from the first, been anxious to show her enthusiasm for the war and her loyalty to her adopted Russia. The huge Catherine Palace at Tsarskoe Selo had been converted into a military hospital and by the end of 1914 eighty-five hospitals in the Petrograd area alone operated under patronage. The Empress who had lain in bed until noon, was now up for Mass at seven, touring hospital wards and — having earned the diploma of Red Cross War Nurse — assisting in the operating theatre. She still found time to write long, passionate letters to Nicholas, and to watch over Alexis. But her efforts undermined her health and by the spring of 1916 she was using a wheelchair when not in public. The politics of war did not initially concern her, but within a few months she had begun gently to chide the Tsar for his unassuming manner. 'Forgive me, precious one,' she wrote in April 1915, 'but you know you are too kind and gentle — sometimes a good loud voice can do wonders and a severe look — do, my love, be more decided and sure of yourself. You know perfectly well what is right.' In this way she saw herself as protecting not only her husband's prerogative, but her son's birthright — 'For Baby's sake we must be firm as otherwise his inheritance will be awful . . .

In the first autumn of the war Rasputin had lost some of his influence at Tsarskoe Selo. Nicholas was angered by his opposition to what he considered a patriotic war. Alexandra was preoccupied with her hospital work. Then, in January 1915, his influence was dramatically restored. Anna Vyrubova, Alexandra's companion, was crushed in a train wreck; dying from multiple injuries she awaited her end, Nicholas and Alexandra beside her. Rasputin, hearing of the accident, rushed to the hospital, charged into her room and stared down at the delirious woman with his mesmeric, frightening eyes. Firmly he commanded her to move and speak. Feebly she did so, 'She will recover, but she will remain a cripple,' he said, turning to the amazed Nicholas and Alexandra. Then he staggered theatrically from the room and collapsed in a wave of dizziness and perspiration.

Rasputin's double life

His reputation and influence restored, Rasputin continued to hold court in his modest St Petersburg apartment, receiving callers who wanted to use his clairvoyant powers or his personal influence, and prepared to pay lavishly in return, with money or by other means. The police, assigned to simultaneously protect and watch him, made careful notes of all his visitors — 'An unknown clergyman brought fish for Rasputin . . . Councillor von Kok brought Rasputin a case of wine . . . Maria Gill, the wife of a Captain in the 145th Regiment slept at Rasputin's . . . About 1 a.m. Rasputin brought an unknown woman back to the house; she spent the night with him . . . Vararova, the actress, slept at Rasputin's' etc. So long as he was undisturbed Rasputin took little interest in politics, but those ministers who crossed him or attempted to challenge his influence with the Imperial Family, he marked out as enemies and, in self-defence, engineered their downfall, regardless of the consequences for Russia. Alexandra, only too willing to draw strength from his flattering reassurances of divine guidance, continued to dismiss the accusations against him as lies. Her deepest concern was to preserve the autocracy for her husband and son. It was Rasputin's also, for the more power his patrons had, the more influence and freedom were available to him and, as a peasant himself, he hated and distrusted the Duma and its representatives, drawn from the landowning, employing classes, the real petty tyrants of peasant Russia.

Disastrous appointment

Alexandra, insecure in her new position as *de facto* ruler of Russia, relied heavily on her *starets* for advice. Skilfully he manoeuvred his enemies out of office, while those who would favour or at least tolerate him received the highest appointments. In the sixteen months after Alexandra took a personal lead in government, Russia had four Prime Ministers, five Ministers of Interior, four Ministers of Agriculture and three ministers of War. Goremykin, the aged retainer of the Tsars, lost control of the Duma completely and, thanks to Rasputin, was replaced by Stürmer, 'an utter non-entity' and 'a false and double-faced man' in the estimation of his colleagues.

Polivanov, the energetic War Minister who had made the spring offensive of 1916 possible, was replaced by the ancient, devoted but incompetent General Shuvaiev. Sazanov, Foreign Minister since 1910, confidant of the Tsar, completely trusted by the Allied Governments, was dismissed over the protests of the British and French ambassadors. To universal amazement, Stürmer was then given the duties of Foreign Minister along with those of Prime Minister. The key Ministry of the Interior, with responsibility for the police, secret service, maintenance of law and order and distribution of food supplies, was ultimately placed in the hands of Protopopov, a charming and apparently efficient liberal, who had been vice-president of the Duma.

Nicholas sanctioned his appointment as a concession to his critics but once in office Protopopov showed himself to be eccentric if not mad, speaking directly to an icon he kept on his desk and uttering prophetic statements at ministerial meetings, as though possessed by a spirit — 'I feel that I shall save Russia. I feel that I alone can save her.' He was, moreover, completely under Rasputin's spell. With Rasputin's guidance Alexandra began to intervene in military affairs, suggesting troop movements, commenting on appointments, confiding top secret information to the *starets,* who boastingly repeated it to anyone who was listening when he was drunk, including, it was discovered, a number of German agents.

The situation becomes desperate

By the autumn of 1916 the Russian situation was becoming desperate. Front line troops lacked shells and cartridges. The railways were in hopeless disorder. Prices were soaring and in response to starvation, strikes and riots grew daily more serious. In the Duma even the right-wing deputies were bitterly critical of the Government and Maklakov, a right-wing liberal, finished a brilliant oration by declaring that 'The old regime and the interests of Russia have parted company.' Quoting from Pushkin, he shouted, 'Woe to that country where only the slave and the liar are close to the throne.'

Nicholas, worn down by strain, his health beginning to suffer, received the same letter of exhortation from Alexandra — 'how long, years, people have told me the same,"Russia loves to feel the whip"— it's their nature . . . How I wish I could pour my will in your veins . . . Be Peter the Great, Ivan the Terrible . . . crush them all under you . . .' Alexandra was by now herself an object of suspicion and hatred. Her brother had a senior rank in the German Army, Stürmer, her protégé, had a German name, Rasputin, it was widely believed, was a German spy. By 1916 even the wounded in the wards began to treat her with disrespect and even rudeness.

Among the Romanov family despera-

Россійскій
Царствующій
домъ...

tion reached the point at which Grand Duke Paul, the Tsar's only surviving uncle, was deputed to beg Nicholas to grant a constitution and a government responsible to the Duma. Nicholas sternly refused, reproaching his uncle for asking him to break his coronation oath to maintain the autocratic power intact for his successors. In the Duma on December 2nd, Purishkevich, a fervent patriot, monarchist and war worker, denounced the 'dark forces' which surrounded the throne — in a thunderous two hour speech which was tumultuously applauded. 'Revolution threatens,' he warned, 'and an obscure *moujik* (peasant) shall govern Russia no longer.' From the visitors' box Prince Felix Yussoupov stared at the speaker in horror and fascination.

Rasputin and his royal puppets — a Russian opposition cartoon.

12

The death of Rasputin

Felix Yussoupov, a slender, beautiful young man of twenty-nine, was sole heir to the largest fortune in Russia. His seven palaces, thirty-seven estates and almost numberless mines, factories and oil wells, were valued at more than £100,000,000. His life was a round of pleasure and debauchery. Opium and transvestism were tried and discarded in search of new diversions. Inevitably Yussoupov was drawn by the magnetic personality of Rasputin and became for a while his closest companion; but when he came to realise the extent of the *starets'* evil influence over the Empress, he resolved that Rasputin must die.

Inspired by Purishkevich, Felix Yussoupov decided that the hour for action had arrived. With Grand Duke Dimitry, son of Grand Duke Paul, they plotted to lure Rasputin to the cellar of the Moika Palace, the ancient Petrograd residence of the Yussoupov family, and then poison him to death. On the night of December 29th Gregory Rasputin, expecting to join a wild party, arrived with his youthful host to find a feast of cakes and dainties spread before him, each dosed with enough cyanide to kill half a dozen men instantly. Rasputin gobbled two and washed them down with two glasses of poisoned Madeira. Nothing happened. Horrified Felix sat for two and a half hours talking and singing with the fuddled priest. In desperation he fled from the room and returned with Dimitry's Browning revolver. At point-blank range he shot Rasputin in the back.

Pronounced dead by a doctor also in on the murder conspiracy, Rasputin, foaming at the mouth, leaped from the cellar floor and threw himself at Yussoupov's throat. The young man fled terrified and, roaring with pain and anger, clambering on all fours, Rasputin pursued him into the darkened courtyard of the palace where Purishkevich brought him down with bullets in the head and shoulder, yards short of the palace gates and then, with the others, beat him to death in the snow. Rolling the corpse in a blue curtain they bound it with rope and pushed it through a hole in the ice of the frozen Neva. Three days later, when the body was recovered, the lungs were filled with water. Gregory

Rasputin, poisoned, shot and beaten into unconsciousness, had actually died by drowning, having partially freed himself from his bonds.

Rasputin's prophecy

Rasputin had known that he was going to die, and in the last weeks of December 1916, dictated the following extraordinary letter to Simanovich, his secretary and confidant:—

'. . . I feel that I shall leave life before January 1st. I wish to make known to the Russian people, to Papa, to the Russian Mother and to the Children, to the land of Russia, what they must understand. If I am killed by common assassins, and especially by my brothers the Russian peasants, you, Tsar of Russia, have nothing to fear, remain on your throne and govern, and your children, they will reign for hundreds of years in Russia . . . But . . . if it was your relations who have wrought my death then no one of your family, that is to say, none of your children or relations, will remain alive for more than two years. They will be killed by the Russian people . . .'

News of Rasputin's death was greeted with rejoicing in Petrograd and his murderers were hailed as heroes. Alexandra was prostrate with grief; Nicholas telegraphed from the front, 'Am horrified, shaken' — not perhaps at the murder itself, but at its effect on his wife and the fact that 'the hands of my kinsmen are stained with the blood of a simple peasant.' Dimitry was ordered on active service to Persia (which enabled him to escape the revolution); Felix was banished to one of his country estates, (from which he fled a year later with a million in jewels and two Rembrandts). Rasputin was buried in a corner of the Imperial Park at Tsarskoe Selo in the presence of the entire Imperial family.

The edge of revolution

Nicholas entered a phase of nervous collapse and kept himself shut up with his family in the Alexander Palace. The year had aged him terribly — he had lost weight, become pallid and wrinkled. His eyes were faded and wandered aimlessly. On his mouth he wore a fixed smile but he bore about him an air of helplessness. Alexandra, his source of strength, was bowed down with the memory of Rasputin's terrible secret prophecy — 'If I die or you desert me, you will lose your son and your crown within six months.'

In the conduct of Russia's Government, Rasputin's death changed nothing. Trepov, successor to Stürmer as Prime Minister, resigned after three months to make way for Golitsyn, an elderly nobody who had served as deputy chairman on one of Alexandra's charity committees, and was appalled at his own appointment. Real power lay in the hands of Protopopov, who scarcely bothered to attend ministerial meetings and faithfully reported to Alexandra each morning how Rasputin had instructed him in his dreams. As the administration began to disintegrate completely both the French and British ambassadors personally pleaded with the Tsar to appoint a government acceptable to the Duma. Rodzianko, the loyal Duma president, spoke in terms so frank that he courted exile to Siberia. Nicholas remained firm and planned his offensive for spring 1917. Protopopov meanwhile began training the city police in the use of machine guns.

13 Revolution: March 1917

By the spring of 1917 Russia was on the edge of total collapse. The Army had taken 15 million men from the farms and food prices had soared. An egg cost four times what it had in 1914, butter five times as much. The severe winter dealt the railways, overburdened by emergency shipments of coal and supplies, the final blow. Russia began the war with 20,000 locomotives; by 1917 9,000 were in service, while the number of serviceable railway wagons had dwindled from half a million to 170,000. Then in February, 1,200 locomotives burst their boilers and nearly 60,000 wagons were immobilized. In Petrograd supplies of flour and fuel all but disappeared. On Thursday, March 8th, Nicholas returned to field headquarters, while in the capital the long-suffering breadlines erupted into violence and pillaged the bakeries. Larger crowds filled the streets on the 9th and by Saturday, 10th, most of Petrograd was on strike. In the streets red banners appeared and the crowds chanted. 'Down with the German woman!' Down with Protopopov! Down with the war!' The Cabinet begged

Revolution — March 1917 — a hoard of flour is 'liberated' from a police-station. It was taken to the Duma for distribution to the poor.

Nicholas to return and offered to resign *en bloc*. Five hundred miles away the Tsar, misinformed by Protopopov that the situation was under control, ordered that firm steps be taken against the demonstrators. For this task the Petrograd garrison was quite unsuitable. The cream of the old regular Army lay in their graves in Poland and Galicia; in Petrograd 170,000 recruits, country boys or older men from the working-class suburbs of the capital itself, remained to keep order under the command of wounded officers invalided from the front, and cadets from the military academies. Many units, lacking both officers and rifles, had never undergone formal training. General Khabalov attempted to put the Tsar's instructions into effect on Sunday morning, March 11th. Despite huge posters ordering people to keep off the streets, vast crowds gathered and were only dispersed after some 200 had been shot dead — though a company of the Volinsky Regiment fired into the air rather than at the mob, and a company of the Pavlovsky Life Guards shot the officer who gave the command to open fire. Nicholas, informed of the situation by the anguished Rodzianko, ordered reinforcements to the capital and suspended the Duma.

The events of one day

It was too late. On Monday, March 12th, the Volinsky Regiment mutinied and was quickly joined by the Semonovsky, the Ismailovsky, the Litovsky and even the legendary Preobrajensky Guard, the oldest and staunchest regiment in the Army, created by Peter the Great himself. The arsenal was pillaged; the Ministry of the Interior, Military Government building, police headquarters, the Law Courts and a score of police stations were put to the torch. By noon the fortress of Peter and Paul, with its heavy artillery, was in the hands of the insurgents. By nightfall 66,000 soldiers had joined the revolution. 'Concessions Inevitable' — demonstrations of the 12th March. Soldiers line the route.

At the Duma Rodzianko, loyal still to the Tsar, attempted to keep control of events and, ignoring the Imperial Decree of suspension, set up a committee to restore law and order in the capital. On that same, remarkable Monday, there arose a second rival assembly, the Soviet of Soldiers' and Workers' Deputies whose cooperation had to be secured if complete anarchy was to be avoided. Housed alongside the Duma in the Tauride Palace, the Petrograd Soviet immediately fell under the domination of its vice-chairman, soon to be nominated Minister of Justice in the new Provincial Government — his name was Kerensky.

Kerensky

Alexander Kerensky was the son of the director of the high school in Simbirsk, an isolated town overlooking the Middle Volga. As a boy he was a fervent believer in both Tsardom and Orthodoxy but as a student in St Petersburg he became involved in politics and was suspended for a speech at a student gathering. Having graduated in law he spent six years defending political prisoners against prosecution by the state, later becoming an outspoken critic of the Government in the Duma. At thirty-six he took command of the March Revolution.

By Tuesday, March 13th, Petrograd was completely in the hands of the revolutionaries and on the following day the Imperial Guard, His Majesty's Regiment, the personal elite bodyguard of the Tsar, and the Marine Guard, who served aboard the Imperial yacht and knew the Tsar and his family personally, all came to swear allegiance to the Duma, headed by grand Duke Cyril, the first of the Romanovs to break his oath of allegiance (and ironically the pretender to the throne until his death in exile in 1938).

At Tsarskoe Selo Alexandra, her son, daughters and faithful servants, waited in fear and ignorance. On the evening of the

'He had the air of a workman in his Sunday clothes . . .' Kerensky reviewing troops.

12th a garbled telegram was sent to the Tsar — 'Concessions inevitable. Street fighting continues. Many units gone over to the enemy. Alix.' At 5 a.m. on Tuesday morning the Imperial train left the front for Tsarskoe Selo; less than twenty-four hours later the train was halted, one hundred miles south of the capital and an officer boarded to inform the Tsar that revolutionary soldiers with machine guns and artillery were blocking the track. Turning west to Pskov the Tsar arrived there to learn of the defection of his personal bodyguard and of the expedition sent ahead under General Ivanov to restore order. Too late Nicholas telegraphed to Rodzianko to offer a government acceptable to the Duma. His reply was swift and dramatic:

'A terrible revolution has broken out, Hatred of the Empress has reached a fever pitch. To prevent bloodshed I have been forced to arrest all the ministers . . . Don't send any more troops. I am hanging by a thread myself. Power is slipping from my hands. The measures you propose are too late. The time for them is gone. There is no return.'

Abdication

Already the Duma and the Soviet had formed the nucleus of a Provisional Government and decided that Nicholas must abdicate. Faced with this demand, which was echoed by his generals; deprived of loyal troops, with his family firmly in the hands of the Provisional Government; fearful of unleashing civil war and opening the way for German conquest — Nicholas had no choice but to submit. Knowing that abdication in favour of Alexis would mean exile and separation from his son, he named his younger brother, Grand Duke Michael, the playboy 'Mishka', as his successor. In his abdication address Nicholas emphasized that it was his patriotism which led him to take this great step:

brought to a victorious end.'

The fall of autocratic Tsardom brought joy to Liberals and Socialists in England and France and made it possible for the USA, the first foreign country to recognize the Provisional Government, to enter the war early in April fighting in an alliance of democracies against an alliance of empires. In Russia the announcement was greeted with many emotions — delight, relief, fear, anger and confusion.

guarantee his safety in the turmoil of Petrograd, the new Tsar, Michael II, the first to bear that name since Michael Romanov founded the dynasty, abruptly abdicated and with that act 304 years of Romanov rule came to an end.

Tsar for a day — Grand Duke Michael.

News from Home — front-line troops greet the overthrow of the Tsar with joy.

'The destiny of Russia, the honour of our heroic Army, the good of the people, the whole future of our dear country demand that whatever it cost, the war should be

Michael, now thirty-nine, was quite unprepared for his sudden elevation to the throne. He was no coward, having won the St George Cross commanding troops in the Carpathians, but when Rodzianko and Kerensky declared themselves unable to

14

Citizen Romanov

On March 22nd, Nicholas, Tsar no longer, referred to contemptuously by the sentries as 'Nicholas Romanov,' was reunited with his family at Tsarskoe Selo. In the arms of his beloved Empress he finally broke down and wept. Surrounded by his guards, confined to their quarters, the Imperial family was rudely 'inspected' on his first evening home. That same night a band of soldiers broke open Rasputin's tomb and, lifting the putrefying corpse with sticks, flung it onto a pyre of logs and drenched it with petrol. The body burned for six hours as Rasputin's ashes were scattered by icy winds.

Imprisoned in their home, the Imperial family was subjected to a host of petty restrictions and insults by their ragged captors. Nevertheless, they, and those servants who had remained faithful to them, bore their lot patiently and drew courage from the personal example of the ex-Tsar who remained calm and dignified amidst all, and even insisted on the children resuming their lessons with himself as tutor in history and geography. Through the newspapers he took a keen

Olga and Tatiana at work in the grounds of Tsarskoe Selo during their imprisonment. Other members of the Imperial Court attend upon them.

'Citizen Romanov.' Nicholas occupies a humble throne in the gardens of Tsarskoe Selo.

interest in the progress of the war, but he could not help reading also how the Press now gleefully printed lurid stories about Rasputin and the Empress, the 'confessions' of former servants and the 'private lives' of the self-styled 'lovers' of the Tsar's four young daughters.

Kerensky's dilemma

Kerensky, at first hostile, visited the captives to interrogate the Empress on charges of 'treasonable, pro-German' activities. Won over by the charm and evident sincerity of the Imperial couple, he began to take a close personal interest in the question of their present security and their future well-being. While Nicholas tended a vegetable garden in the Imperial Park and sawed logs for exercise, Kerensky began to search for a way to ensure the safety of the Imperial family, and as a first step used his position as Minister of Justice to introduce a law abolishing capital punishment. This he knew would help forestall demands for the Tsar's execution.

In London George V expressed his anxiety at the peril of his cousin. Lloyd George, however, was hostile to the Tsar and so was British public opinion. His Majesty's Government made a tentative offer of asylum and then withdrew it under the pretext that the safe passage of the Tsar and his family over U-Boat infested waters could not be guaranteed. While the British vacillated and Kerensky cast anxiously around for some way of releasing

Nicholas and his entourage from their precarious situation, the course of history was abruptly changed by the arrival at the Finland Station in Petrograd of a new leader for the Soviet — Lenin.

Lenin

Vladimir Ilyich Ulyanov, known as Volodya to his family, as Lenin to posterity, was born in Simbirsk in 1870 and attended the school where Kerensky's father was headmaster. His final report recorded that he was:

'Very gifted, always neat and assiduous, Ulyanov was first in all his subjects, and upon completing his studies received a gold medal as the most deserving pupil with regard to his ability, progress and behaviour. Neither in the school, nor outside, has a single instance been observed when he has given a cause for dissatisfaction by word or by deed . . .'

When this was written Lenin's character had already been transformed by the sudden death of his father and the execution of his elder brother for his part in a futile plot to assassinate Alexander III. Expelled from the University of Kazan for his revolutionary activities Lenin took up and abandoned farming and then completed a four year legal course in a single year, passing out top in his class. Practising as a lawyer, he joined a Marxist study group in St Petersburg and in 1895 toured Europe, meeting Plekhanov and other exiled revolutionaries. On his return he began to

organize strikes and distribute forbidden literature, for which he was arrested and after a year in jail, dispatched to a relatively comfortable exile in Siberia where he lived happily for three years with his young wife, hunting in the woods, translating the Webbs' *Theory and Practice of Trade Unionism* into Russian and working on his own monumental volume *The Development of Capitalism in Russia*. Exile in Europe followed, and with it the editorship of a

'The Hammer of the Proletariat strikes'.

revolutionary newspaper *Iskra* (the Spark). At the stormy London conference of the Social Democratic Party in 1903 Plekhanov's less radical followers, to be known as the Mensheviks ('minorityites') lost to Lenin's majority faction. Dedicated to the creation of an elite party claiming to seize power by force, their name was to become more famous — the Bolsheviks.

By May Lenin had begun to gain ascendancy in the Soviet and coined an irresistible slogan which combined the deepest wishes of the war-weary Russian people: 'Peace, Land, All Power to the Soviet.' By forcing Miliukov, Guchkov and Prince Lvov from office, the Soviet raised Kerensky to become simultaneously Prime Minister and Minister for War. Aided by massive loans from his western allies Kerensky launched the Russian armies into the attack. Initial success was reversed by a vigorous German counter-attack. Retreat turned into rout and on July 16th, 1917, half a million peopled marched through Petrograd, demanding an end to war and the Provisional Government. The rising was stifled by the Provisional Government's circulation of a rumour that Lenin was a German agent and he was forced to flee into Finland disguised as a fireman on a locomotive.

At the Finland Station — an idealized Soviet impression of Lenin's arrival, April 3rd, 1917.

15

Siberia

Marooned — the Imperial family on the roof of the former Governor's residence of Tobolsk.

Kerensky, shaken by the narrowness of his victory, decided to move the Imperial family away from turbulent Petrograd to Tobolsk, an isolated town in western Siberia. The subject was never discussed at Cabinet meetings and Kerensky, who personally arranged all the details of the transfer, himself supervised the departure of the 'Japanese Red Cross Mission' train which pulled out of Tsarsko Selo with the entire Imperial family, the ladies and gentlemen of their suite, thirty servants and two pet spaniels.

Arriving in Tobolsk after four days by train and two days by river steamer, the Imperial entourage installed itself in the Governor's residence, their house for the next eight months. Surrounded by a high wooden fence the family took exercise in the gardens of the white two-storey house, while outside the peasants stood on tiptoe to glimpse them or sent presents of fruit and flowers.

In Petrograd events moved even faster than Kerensky had anticipated. When General Kornilov, Commander-in-Chief of the Army, decided to march on Petrograd, smash the Bolshevik-dominated Soviet and establish a military dictatorship, Kerensky was forced to appeal to the Bolsheviks and arm the workers to avoid a complete Right-wing counter coup. Ironically, Kornilov's threat evaporated when his Army began to fraternize with the 'Red Guard' workers' militia, and Lenin returned from exile to lead the Bolsheviks in an armed rising.

The 'November Revolution'

On November 6th the Revolution began. The cruiser, *Aurora,* flying the red flag, anchored in the Neva opposite the Winter Palace and squads of armed workers occupied stations, bridges, telephone exchanges and public buildings. The following morning Kerensky left unmolested for what became fifty years exile, while his colleagues sat in the Winter Palace guarded by a battalion of women soldiers

The Bolshevik Revolution — sailors land from the cruiser *Aurora.*

and a troop of cadets. At 2.10 a.m. on November 8th, after a brief and inaccurate bombardment from the *Aurora,* the remnant of the Provisional Government surrendered all power to the Soviet. In Tobolsk Nicholas followed these events with interest but as yet no alarm. He continued to underestimate Lenin's importance but already began to feel that his abdication had done Russia more harm than good. In the meantime he and his family must occupy themselves with keeping warm — the temperature in December was 68 degrees below zero. Soviet domination now meant more spiteful restrictions. The Tsar was forbidden to wear his officer's epaulettes and the sentries scrawled lewd drawings on the fence to offend his daughters. On March 1st the family was put on soldiers' rations, which meant parting with ten devoted servants and giving up even butter and coffee as luxuries. What kept them going was the belief that help was at hand.

Even before the Bolshevik take-over, strong monarchist organizations had begun to plan the rescue of the Imperial family. In the event none succeeded, because the Tsar insisted on not being separated from his family, because there were too many groups working at cross-purposes to one another and because eventually they accepted Boris Soloviev as their leader and he, the son-in-law of Rasputin, absconded with the very considerable sum of money which had been entrusted to him.

The 'humiliating' peace treaty

On March 3rd, 1918, in the town of Brest-Litovsk, headquarters of the German Eastern Front, a Bolshevik delegation signed a peace treaty so humiliating to Russia that one general, after observing the ceremony, went out and shot himself.

The Bolshevik Revolution — the storming of the Winter Palace, a still from a Soviet propaganda film made in 1927 to celebrate the 10th anniversary of the fall of Tsardom. Many of the 'stars' had taken part in the actual events.

Under the terms of the settlement Russia renounced nearly all of the territory she had won in the past two centuries — including Poland, Finland, the Baltic States, the Ukraine, the Crimea and most of the Caucasus — 400,000 square miles of territory with a population of 60 million people, more than one third of the population of the Empire. At Tobolsk Nicholas was overwhelmed with shame and grief and appalled that 'the Emperor William and the German Government could stoop to shake hands with these miserable traitors.'

Soon the arrival of Commissar Vasily Vaslevich Yakovlev with 150 soldiers gave the Imperial family a more personal source of anxiety. Although courteous and cultured the Commissar seemed to represent a vague and undefined threat. Three days after his arrival he took half the family from Tobolsk in peasant carts bound for the railway 200 miles away and ultimately headed for Omsk. Sixty miles from Omsk their train was surrounded by troops and Yakovlev was forced to take his charges to Ekaterinburg and hand them over to the custody of the Ural Soviet, in the most bitterly anti-monarchist area in Russia. When Yakovlev contacted his superiors in Moscow, the Moscow Soviet claimed to have lost control of the situation. Whether this was in fact so or whether the actions of the authorities at Ekaterinburg were in fact authorized from Moscow we cannot know.

16 Ekaterinburg

At Ekaterinburg the reunited Imperial family was incarcerated in 'The House of Special Purpose' and closely guarded night and day. Coarse diet, confinement, insults and obscene gestures by their captors added to their discomfort. When Nagorny, the faithful sailor servant of the Tsarevich, argued too often with guards over the needs of the sick child, he was finally taken away and shot. On July 4th the unkempt worker guards of the local Soviet were replaced by ten members of the Cheka, the Bolshevik secret police. The government in Moscow had begun to panic as Bolshevik power was suddenly challenged on all sides. British and American troops had landed in Murmansk; in the Ukraine Generals Alexeiev, Kornilov and Deniken had organized a White Volunteer Army with the cooperation of the Don Cossacks; in Siberia, an independent Czech Legion, composed of 45,000 prisoners of war, was moving rapidly towards Ekaterinburg. In these circumstances Moscow gave up the plan for a public trial of the Tsar and authorized the Ural Soviet to take the matter of the Romanovs into their own hands. On July 12th,

The House of Special Purpose',
Ekaterinburg 1918.

believing that the Czechs were barely a week away, it was decided to shoot the entire family and destroy their bodies.

Murder

At midnight on July 16th-17th the Imperial family was ordered to dress and assemble in the cellar of the house which was their prison. Here Alexandra, Nicholas and Alexis sat, waiting, so they thought, to be moved to a place of safety, out of range of the expected fighting. Behind them stood the four girls, Dr Botkin, their physician, Trupp, the valet, Kharitonov, the cook and Demidova, the maid. Suddenly Yurovsky entered the room with the entire Cheka squad, armed with revolvers. Nicholas and Alexandra each died from a single shot. Olga, Tatiana, Marie, Botkin, Kharitonov and Trupp were hit several times and died quickly. Alexis, Anastasia and Demidova survived the first volley and were finished off with bayonets and rifle butts. The bodies were then taken

to a disused mine shaft fourteen miles away, hacked to pieces with axes and saws and burned, the process taking three days. The ashes and residue were thrown into a pool of water at the bottom of the mine shaft. The Whites took Ekaterinburg eight days after the murder.

In January 1919, on the orders of the 'White' Admiral Kolchak, Nicholas Sokolov, a trained legal investigator, conducted a search inquiry, assisted by the tutors, Gilliard and Gibbs. Among the articles found were the belt buckles of the Tsar and Tsarevich, an emerald cross, a diamond badge, a pearl earring, a spectacle case all belonging to Alexandra, three small icons worn by the Grand Duchesses, together with their shoebuckles, six sets of women's corsets, a severed finger belonging to a middle-aged woman — and the metal case in which Nicholas always carried a portrait of Alexandra.

A year after the murder twenty Social Revolutionaries were arrested by the Soviet Government and charged with murdering the Tsar in order to discredit the Bolsheviks. Five were executed. No mention was made of the fate of the rest of the family.

Striking down the hydra of Tsarism.